Countries We Come From

Afghanistan

by Ariel Factor Birdoff

Consultant: Marjorie Faulstich Orellana, PhD
Professor of Urban Schooling
University of California, Los Angeles

BEARPORT PUBLISHING

New York, New York

Credits

Cover, © Travel Stock/Shutterstock and © brusinski/iStock; TOC, © Metropolitan Museum of Art/CC0; 4, © Iakov Filimonov/Shutterstock; 5L, © Alex Treadway/robertharding/AGE Fotostock; 5R, © Marion Kaplan/Alamy; 7, © Rashad Mammadov/Shutterstock; 8, © mbrand85/Shutterstock; 9T, © Arsal_Photography/Shutterstock; 9B, © Dermot Tatlow/Panos Pictures/Redux Pictures; 10L, © National Geographic Image Collection/Alamy; 10–11, © nikm4860/Shutterstock; 12, © wrangle/iStock; 13T, © Milan Zygmunt/Shutterstock; 13B, © abzerit/iStock; 14T, © Historical Views/AGE Fotostock; 14B, © Aurora Photos/Alamy; 15, © The History Collection/Alamy; 16, © Erwin Lux/CC BY-SA 4.0; 17T, © Rob Leyland/Shutterstock; 17B, © Mohammad Ismail/Reuters/Newscom; 18, © MivPiv/iStock; 19, © ton koene/Alamy; 20, © PJF Military Collection/Alamy; 21, © Ton Koene/AGE Fotostock; 22T, © JordiStock/iStock; 22B, © Fanfo/Shutterstock; 23, © talynshererphoto/iStock; 24T, © ME_Photography/Shutterstock; 24B, © Oleksandr Rupeta/Alamy; 25, © timsimages/Alamy; 26, © Danita Delimont/Alamy; 27, © Album/Alamy; 28L, © Omar Sobhani/Reuters/Newscom; 28–29, © MehmetO/Shutterstock; 30T, © Oleg_Mit/Shutterstock, © Andrey Lobachev/Shutterstock, and © Fat Jackey/Shutterstock; 30B, © PA Images/Alamy; 31 (T to B), © Luks23/Shutterstock, © Mark Time Author/Shutterstock, © MisoKnitl/iStock, Public Domain, © fckncg/Shutterstock, and © Prazis Images/Shutterstock; 32, © Boris15/Shutterstock.

Publisher: Kenn Goin
Senior Editor: Joyce Tavolacci
Creative Director: Spencer Brinker
Design: Debrah Kaiser
Photo Researcher: Thomas Persano

Library of Congress Cataloging-in-Publication Data

Names: Birdoff, Ariel Factor, author.
Title: Afghanistan / by Ariel Factor Birdoff.
Description: New York, New York: Bearport Publishing Company, Inc., [2020] | Series: Countries we come from | Includes bibliographical references and index.
Identifiers: LCCN 2019010085 (print) | LCCN 2019010403 (ebook) | ISBN 9781642805789 (ebook) | ISBN 9781642805246 (library)
Subjects: LCSH: Afghanistan—Juvenile literature.
Classification: LCC DS351.5 (ebook) | LCC DS351.5 .B535 2020 (print) | DDC 958.1—dc23
LC record available at https://lccn.loc.gov/2019010085

For more information, write to Bearport Publishing Company, Inc., 45 West 21st Street, Suite 3B, New York, New York 10010. Printed in the United States of America.

10 9 8 7 6 5 4 3 2 1

Contents

STRIKING

STRONG

Colorful

Welcome to Afghanistan!
Afghanistan is a country in Asia.
It's about the same size as Texas.

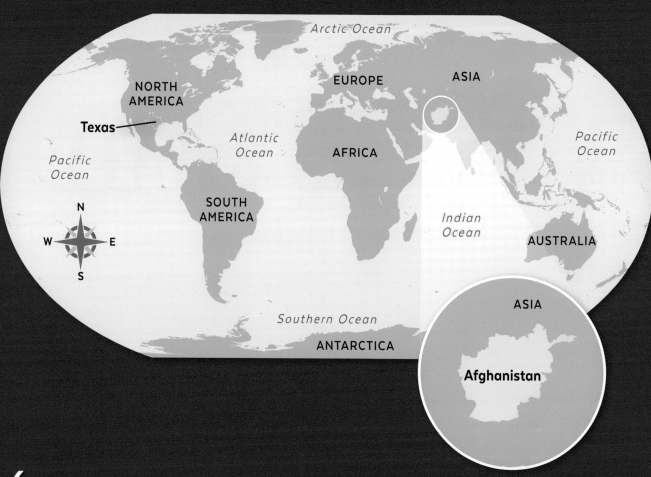

More than 34 million people live in Afghanistan. They're called Afghans.

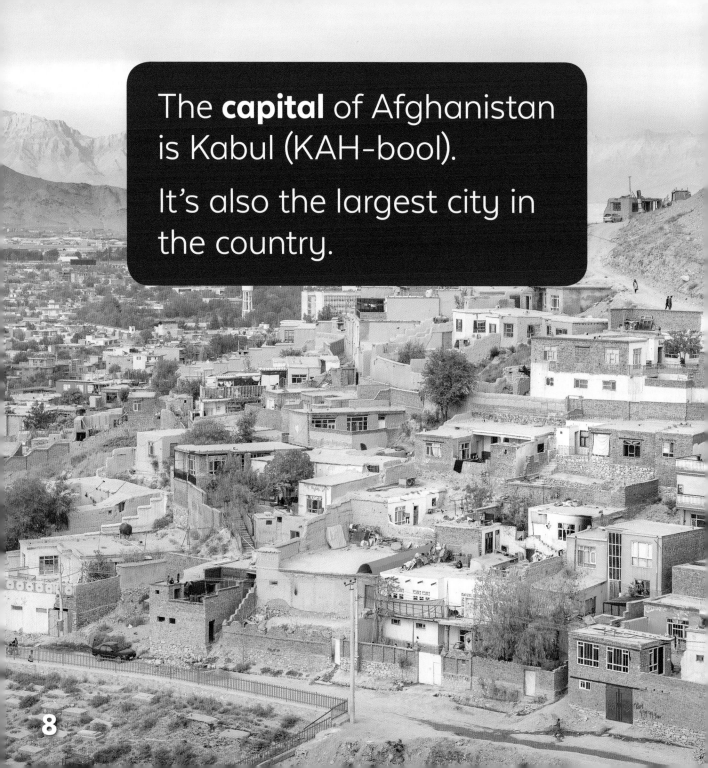

The **capital** of Afghanistan is Kabul (KAH-bool).

It's also the largest city in the country.

Kabul is a blend of old and new buildings.

It has many beautiful gardens.

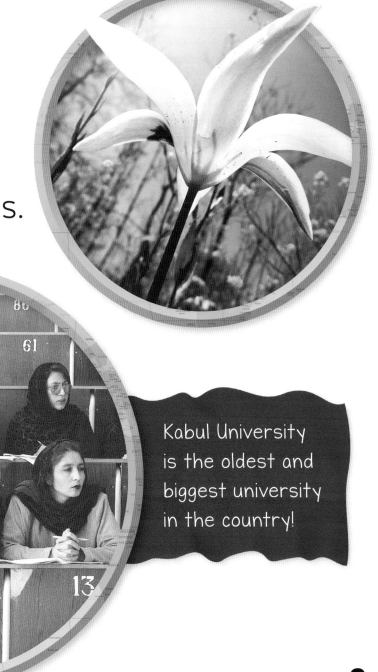

Kabul University is the oldest and biggest university in the country!

Afghanistan has mountains, deserts, and **plains**.

The Hindu Kush Mountains cover much of the country.

Most Afghan people live in the valleys between the mountains.

There are many rivers in Afghanistan. The country's longest river is the Amu Darya.

Unique animals can be found in Afghanistan.

There are wild goats called markhor (mar-KORE).

They have huge, twisting horns.

There are also snow leopards and unusual lizards.

toad-headed agama lizard

The snow leopard is the national animal of Afghanistan.

13

Afghanistan has a long history.

More than 50,000 years ago, people settled there.

They made mud-brick buildings and pottery.

Years later, different tribes fought to control the land.

The tribes included the Pashtun, Tajik, Hazara, and Uzbek.

From 1979 to 1989, the Soviet Union ruled Afghanistan.

The **Taliban** came to power in 1996.

They set up harsh rules that hurt women and girls.

Afghan fighters in 1987

The Taliban also helped **terrorist** groups.

The United States went to war, driving the Taliban from power in 2001.

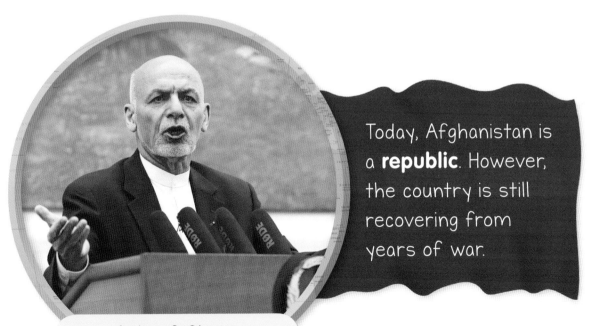

Today, Afghanistan is a **republic**. However, the country is still recovering from years of war.

Ashraf Ghani, Afghanistan's president

Most Afghans are Muslim.

Muslim people follow the religion of Islam.

They worship in **mosques**.

the Blue Mosque
in Mazar-i-Sharif

Muslims pray five times a day. They often kneel on rugs when they pray.

The two main languages of Afghanistan are Dari and Pashto.

This is how you say *good morning* in Dari:

Sobh baxir (SOHB bah-HAR)

This is how you say *good morning* in Pashto:

Sahaar mo pa khayr (sah-HAR mo pah KHAR)

Both Dari and Pashto use the Arabic alphabet.

دنرخ ولسوالی
NARKH DISTRICT

21

Afghan food is full of flavor!

A favorite dish is called *kabuli palaw*.

It's made with rice, raisins, carrots, and lamb.

kabuli palaw

aushak

Aushak is a tasty
meat dumpling
served with yogurt.

Afghanistan is famous for its handmade carpets.

The rugs are often made from sheep's wool.

Weavers cover them with graceful designs.

Afghan rugs are passed down from parents to children.

Afghanistan is also known for its beautiful poetry.

Thursday is poetry night!

Family and friends gather to read their favorite poems.

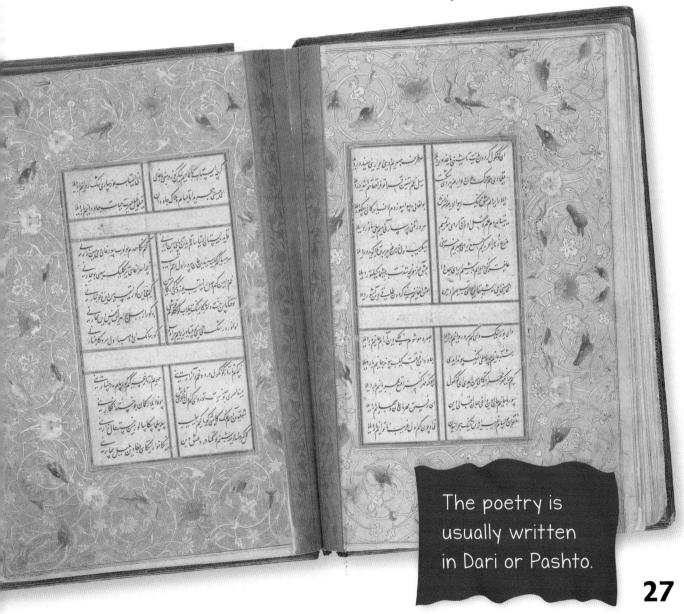

The poetry is usually written in Dari or Pashto.

The wildest sport in Afghanistan is *Buzkashi* (booz-KAH-she).

In the game, horseback riders try to grab a dead goat or calf.

Then, they carry it across a goal!

Afghans also enjoy soccer and wrestling.

Fast Facts

Capital city: Kabul

Population of Afghanistan:
About 34 million

Main languages:
Dari and Pashto

Money: Afghani

Major religion: Islam

Neighboring countries:
China, Iran, Pakistan, Tajikistan,
Turkmenistan, and Uzbekistan

Cool Fact: Afghans celebrate
the New Year, or Nowruz, on
the first day of spring!

capital (KAP-uh-tuhl) the city where a country's government is based

mosques (MOSKS) Muslim places of worship

plains (PLAYNZ) large, flat areas of land

republic (rih-PUB-lick) a government where the leader is elected by the people

Taliban (TAH-luh-ban) a strict religious group in Afghanistan

terrorist (TER-ur-ist) relating to the use of violence and fear to achieve certain goals

Index

Read More

Juarez, Christine. *Afghanistan (Countries).* Mankato, MN: Capstone (2013).

Murray, Julie. *Afghanistan (Explore the Countries).* Pinehurst, NC: Buddy Books (2016).

Learn More Online

To learn more about Afghanistan, visit
www.bearportpublishing.com/CountriesWeComeFrom

About the Author

Ariel Factor Birdoff lives in New York City with her husband. She is a school outreach librarian for the New York Public Library's MyLibraryNYC program. Traveling is one of her favorite things to do.